The Magick

Persuade, Cont
with the For

Corwin Hargrove

CONTENTS

The Workings of Influence

Powerful people get where they are by influencing others. Every time you influence people to join you, adore you, work with you or support your ideas, you've taken one more step toward success. Without influence, you can be manipulated and dragged unwillingly through life in a state of confusion and resentment. Being able to influence others, you take back control. Magick can give you the power of influence.

Everybody is trying to influence you, one way or another. And you try to influence others. You want to be liked, respected, employed. You want to sell, to convince, to be admired and adored. It's all about influence.

This book gives you the keys to magickal influence, so that you can use supernatural forces of darkness to change hearts and minds. Working with angels, demons, ancient spirits and gods, you access many powers. The book won't tell you how to create rapport, charm, and charisma. There are other books that can teach you those skills. This book gives you the magick.

There are 23 rituals to influence individuals and groups. You can create trust, convince somebody that you are right, make somebody find you attractive, and even make somebody care about you. The magick can make another person see you as a leader. When you want to cause disruption, you can sow the seeds of doubt in somebody's mind, so that what once seemed certain becomes uncertain. The magick can create unease, confusion, mistrust and even hatred between people that you know. These rituals can inspire loyalty, or make somebody confess what they have held back from you. There are rituals to make loud people quiet, to silence gossip and to make an unwanted neighbor move away. The rituals can be used to make people fear you, or you can project authority, trustworthiness, and charisma.

These powers can be used within family situations as readily as they can be used to gain an advantage in business or politics. They can be used to solve seemingly small problems, such as noisy neighbors, or to land the promotion you've deserved for years, or undermine your competition, or convince the skeptical to fund your projects. By changing the way people see you, and each other, you can manipulate reality.

If you think it's wrong to influence, or evil to perform magick for your own benefit, then please go buy a book on mindfulness. If you're scared of demons, skip the second half of the book. If you've got no idea what this magick is, but get the feeling that magick might work, this is going to be fun. If you've been using magick for years, you've probably seen it all before but, you never know, this might work for you.

The first half of this book is all about magick that originates in the tradition of magick that was explored in the Greek Magickal Papyri. The magick in those texts was sourced from older traditions, including Jewish magick, and was corrupted and distorted, modified and evolved. But the papyri are a great source of magick, if you take the time to understand the workings and get past the omissions, confusions and the bits that are plain useless. This strand of magick is called The Magick of the Calls.

The second half of this book works with the Goetic demons. It's a method that's simplified, without losing the dark charm of magick. You feel the energy of the demons, and they influence the people you ask them to influence. There are so many books about these demons that I'm almost embarrassed to put something else out there, but I hope that I've got something you're going to like. It's a quick, easy way to get the demons to respond, without too much trouble, and without being so simple that it feels diluted. I refer to this magick as Demonic Influence, just to keep things simple.

You can purchase the original magickal texts and sources, and unearth a few translations, and collect stacks of theoretical books, and then test it out with different methods and you'll probably invent the same rituals that are in this book. Or something quite like them. But I've done the work for you. That's what you're paying your hard-earned dollars for. I offer you my time and experience as a practicing occultist. In return, I give you magick that works. That's the pact we have made, you and I, with this book. I write, you read, you do the magick.

There are many occultists that belong to long traditions and respected magickal orders. They have great tales to tell, and wear glorious robes and hats and that sort of thing. I am not one of them. I have belonged to a few groups, and I've learned from some great people, but most of the time I work by myself. I do not set myself up as a grand and famous occultist. But I am a *practicing occultist* and I think that matters more than belonging to any amazing lodge of darkness and mystery. I've seen and experienced wonderful and terrible things. I've experienced magick that works. What's on offer in this book can be called terrible or wonderful, depending on your point of view. I hope that it's wonderful, and gets you what you want.

All magick of influence is evil, so they say. But the world is a network of influence. Every act is an act of influence. When you smile at a stranger, you influence their feelings. When you attempt to get more sales for a product with clever advertising, you influence the masses to defeat your competitors. When you persuade, spread doubt, create an aura of charm, or develop a personal mythology, you influence others to bring about change.

I look for the good in people, but I also see the bad. Without the ability to influence those around me, I would be a victim of circumstance and a victim of people. I choose to take the upper hand, to control those who upset me, to persuade those who need to be more cooperative, and to weaken those who pester and undermine.

When you remain subject to the influence of others, you are a victim of life. When you take control and influence others as you choose, this gives you the power to be authentic. The magick in this book can be used recklessly and to cause harm, or it can be used shrewdly and graciously to steer events in a way that meets with your desire.

It could be claimed that we like to be influenced. To be seduced by a charming person is not the same thing as date rape; it's a cooperative act where influence is accepted willingly by the one being seduced. To be persuaded to buy a car from a salesperson is not to be coerced, because you went to the showroom to buy a car, and you wanted to be sold that car. To have an employee convince you that she deserves a promotion is not a trick, but a way for the employee to show what she is capable of. And so what?

This is a book of dark magick, so let's not worry about the morals too much. You make a decision to influence somebody because that's *what you want to do*. You want to change how they think and feel. But, at the same time what I say about influence being partly cooperative is true. I'm not being moralistic, but I want you to avoid the trap of thinking you're a dangerous and deadly dark magician. Some folks really get off on appearing scary, but that's not the point of this magick. The point of the magick is to get what you want. You put your needs first; you get what you want. But the magick can also be used for good. Influence a bad person to quit being cruel, and you're a hero. But, you know, don't get a hero complex. I'm telling you to keep your feet on the ground because when this magick works, and when you're able to sway people and bend their will and weaken them, it can go to your head. You're in danger. Not from demons, but from your own petty need to look impressive. So don't show off, don't get caught up on how powerful you are. Every time that happens, you end up flat on your face and looking like a moron. Be cool. Use the magick and chill out. You got what you wanted, so don't act like a douche about it.

Influence magick works, but if you go in too hard, all guns blazing, you might awaken resistance in the other person. Be subtle and patient. Make the least amount of change you need to make. That way you are more likely to get the person to change, to succumb to your influence, than if you try to change everything. If your boss is treating you badly, and you want him to stop, do a ritual to get him to stop. But that's all. You don't need to change him into a better man and make him nicer to his kids. Just get him to lighten up when he's around you. That degree of effect is easy to accomplish. Changing him completely is just about impossible, so don't even try.

Look at what you want, and do magick to make the change you need that will make your life better.

Ever done a seduction spell to make somebody fall completely in love with you, and then been stuck in a heavy, heavy relationship? Way better to use a ritual to get that first date, and then see how things go.

Ever done a ritual to get a massive promotion, and then found you're out of your depth because you should have asked for a *reasonable* promotion? It happens. Overkill is not as smart as moderation. Minimalist magick is the way to go. So let me say it again so that you can't miss it: *Make the least amount of change you need to make.*

I mean, get what you want. If the change you want is pretty big, then don't hang back, go big. But don't go for big results because you haven't had a good think about it. Have a good think. Know what you want to happen, and then make it happen.

I can't explain everything, so don't expect me to. How can magick possibly work, in an age of smartphones and reality tv? How can we conceivably connect to the world of the supernatural and mystical, when we are drowned in information and entertainment? How can a sane person ignore the scientists we trust, and decide to perform a ritual? Because you *know*. You know that magick is real.

And that is all I need to say about that. You can work out the big questions for yourself. As for me, I'll just tell you the influence rituals that have worked for me.

This is not a long book. I'm not going to waste my time telling you stories about how well it works, or who I've influenced, or how wonderful it is to be a glorious occultist. I like magick because it works. If you like magick too, use the book, use the magick. It's short and gets the job done as fast as possible, because I've got better things to do than keep writing about my beliefs, and *you* want to get on with the magick. This super-fast, super-shallow approach to magick is all the rage these days, and that's a good thing. Doing magick is better than reading about it, so get the reading done so you can get to the good bit. Actually doing magick!!!

Actually doing magick is, on the face of it, madness. But it's an enjoyable madness, and if you've got the guts to do this, you feel the truth, the reality of the universe, and you know you're connected to something bigger and... I'm starting to sound like an occultist. Let's move on. The magick works. You'll see for yourself.

Before the Magick

In traditional magick, it was *all* about the preparation, with months of fasting and cleansing. In modern magick, people don't prepare at all. Shut the door, hope nobody's listening, rush out your ritual and *boom*, your wish is granted. Well, sure...

People hate preparation. You don't want to spend three weeks gathering herbs, so I get that. Its why I called this chapter *Before the Magick*, rather than preparation. If I called it Preparation, you'd skip ahead. Don't skip ahead. If you do, you'll then wonder why the magick didn't work, and you'll blame the magick when it's actually you that couldn't summon up the discipline to prepare. So, suck it up. Here's the truth: I've found that *some* preparation is worthwhile.

Look, it's pretty easy. You don't have to spend a week in a sweat lodge or collect any herbs, and there are absolutely no crystals involved at all. The only thing you need to do is spend some time achieving a degree of purification.

Purification can involve lots of fasting and confession, avoiding sex for weeks and that sort of thing. It's meant to make you more appealing to the spirits. It sounds a bit old-fashioned, but look at it this way; you can't get out of bed, stuff some breakfast down and smoke a cigarette, while sipping at your coffee and expect the great and glorious spirits of magick to give a damn about you. Sort yourself out and get in a state that shows some respect for magick. It makes sense.

This is my guide to purification, and it works for all the magick in this book:

Don't have sex for three days before the ritual, and that includes sex with yourself. It sharpens your mind and intensifies your will. It's not fun, but it works. How much do you want this magickal result?

If you need to use the magick in an emergency, and don't have three days in which to abstain, try to do the magick some hours after you have sex. You don't want to get out of bed, sweaty and steaming with satisfaction, and call on the spirits. You'd be too relaxed. It doesn't work well. Abstain for three days if you can, and wait another hour after the magick before you have sex again.

Before the ritual, shower and put on fresh clothes. Some occultists like robes, but I feel like a dick when I see myself in the mirror wearing a robe. I shower, wash my hair, I put on fresh clothes, I do the magick, I take the 'magick clothes' off and put them in the wash and put my civvies back on.

What if you're at work? What if it's the middle of the night? OK, showering and changing clothes is the ideal. If you can't do that, then at least wash your hands and face. Take off your glasses, your jacket. Make it feel like a purification even if it isn't. Ideally, shower and do the rest, but if not, do what you can.

Skip a meal. Yeah, I know that's a big ask. Have you seen how many dieting books there are? Thousands. And if any of those books said, 'Skip one meal a day,' you can imagine the shitstorm. Nobody likes to skip a meal. But how much do you want this magick to work? If you do want it to work, skip breakfast or dinner or whatever meal might leave you feeling full and satisfied when it comes to ritual time. And skip other comforts such as coffee. You think a cup of coffee wakes you up, but it pacifies you. You want to be wired on yourself, on your need, so fast for one meal. You don't want to be too comfortable.

When the ritual's done, eat what you want, straight away. When you're fasting, don't stop drinking water for obvious reasons. It should go without saying that you should only skip a meal if you're healthy enough to do so, and you know, check with your doctor first. If you can't skip a meal for medical reasons, or because you feel like you're going to pass out, try your best to eat long before the ritual, so that you are approaching hunger, rather than feeling stuffed to the windpipe with cream cakes when it's time for your ritual.

If you shave any part of your body, it should be clean-shaven. In some of the traditions connected to this magick, you were advised to shave all body hair. When I first worked this magick, in the eighties, body hair was still everywhere, and you only shaved your pubic hair if you were sexually adventurous or had some sort of skin condition. Modern times bring change, and young people routinely shave all their body hair. Don't worry about this one, but if it appeals, go ahead, shave it all off during your shower.

You can take a bath instead, of course, but I find it a bit too dreamy and relaxing, whereas a shower invigorates. You want to be relaxed but focused, and a sleepy bath might make you too zoned out. Your choice.

Who wants to prepare when you can just do magick? Do this right and the magick's going to work. Miss it out, and you'll wish you'd taken some extra time to get it right.

14

Protection

The magick in this book comes from two different traditions, and they, in turn, are derived from many other traditions. But you can use the same purification and protection magick in both. The essence of protection is similar in so many traditions, and what I offer here is so ancient that it is perfect for both systems.

If you've got your own ideas about protection, and you want to call down specific angels, and all that, then that's up to you. But I will say that going over the top with protection can make you look more afraid than if you go boldly into the magick.

Whatever protection you use, don't get carried away with the idea that a magick circle is going to save you from all harm. The quality and intelligence of your magick are more important than the circle. If you incite hatred in somebody who lives in your house, you get to live with that. If you cause your boss to lose the trust of his employees, and then the company goes bust, that's your problem. You don't need protecting from demons. You need protection from stupidity. So don't be stupid and you'll be safe.

When you're ready to begin your ritual, obtain a small handful of flour and salt. If you can't sprinkle flour on the floor, just use salt. You can vacuum it up later and nobody will know. This is so much easier than scratching a circle into the floor.

Face East and hold both your hands out in front of you. I'll assume you're right-handed. Your left hand is holding the flour and salt, so it's a closed fist, facing the ceiling. Your right hand is right next to it. You take a pinch of flour and salt in your right hand and sprinkle it as you move slowly around, on the spot, anti-clockwise. That means you turn to the left. You're staying in the same place, but your arms are describing a circle. The flour and salt may even form a visible circle around you. Doesn't matter if they don't. When the salt in your right hand runs out, take another pinch and continue, until you're facing East again.

As you do this, you need to say the divine name IAO, over and again. This is said like EEEEE-AHHH-OHHHH, and it should be said with pride and strength. You've started your magick, and you are calling spirits to be aware of you, but delineating a boundary that they cannot cross.

With that done you move on to speak the words of the ritual, as described in each chapter. When the ritual's over, all you do it step out of the circle

The circle isn't just protection, but binds you to this moment, a magickal moment where you state your will to the spirits. It's short and simple, and might not feel dramatic enough for you, but it will work if you trust that it will work.

Part 1: The Magick of the Calls

The first part of this book looks at calls to gods, angels, and other spirits. (Angels are mighty powers that act as a powerful force. They don't sit on clouds doing good deeds. They are an important part of forceful magick)

For each ritual, you will be told when to perform the ritual. You might have been told an exact timing, such as a full moon, or something vague like, 'Start on a Thursday.' In all cases, you will be told to use the magick at a particular planetary hour. It might say, 'Perform at the third hour on a Tuesday during a waxing moon.' That means you work out when the third planetary hour falls, after sunrise, on any Tuesday when the moon is waxing. This takes some work, but not too much.

Read through the following twelve rituals and see which you want to use. Read the ritual, get used to how it sounds and feels. After the rituals, there are two important chapters that show you how to work out the timing and the correct pronunciation. Read through the rituals first and then work out the details you need to get started.

For each and every ritual, do the purification and protection described in the previous chapters, and then follow out the ritual instructions. At the end of the ritual, you step out of the circle and do something more normal than magick, to bring you back down to earth.

Lots has been said about lusting for result, which means you try to forget about the magick after it's done, but it's not too big a deal if your magick is powerful. Don't spend hours thinking about the magick, don't be impatient for the result, but don't try to banish the magick from your mind. You can think about it, so long as you don't spend hours doubting it. That's simple enough.

Change an Individual's Mind

Use this ritual when somebody you know personally thinks one thing, and you want them to think something else. This might be something you argue over, or something you've never even discussed.

Work this ritual on any night when the moon is waning. Perform the ritual during the Sixth Hour of the night. Perform the usual purification and protection, and then say:

"AY-OWE-TH, AY-OO-TH, AH-OTH, hear me, as I say the name AY-OWE-TH, AY-OO-TH, AH-OTH, the one who makes the gods lie down, who brings demons forth and compels angels to complete their work. Hear me as I call AY EH EE EYE OH YOU EYE AY YOEH EH AY OO OH YEH EE OO EYE AH. This is the name that answers, and this is the name I have called.

I call on you, great angel Corborbath of this hour. By the words BAI SOL BAI I call on the great God Sekmet to watch over this ritual.

I call to you, great angel Corborbath. I ask that you change the mind of _____."

You now name the person whose mind you want to change. And then, in your own words, give a clear, brief description of the situation as it is now and how you want it to change.

Then say, "Great angel Corborbath, I give thanks for your help. As you came in peace, go in peace."

Create Rapport with Somebody

Use this when you know you will be spending time with a specific individual in the coming days. Ideally, perform it one day before you meet. The effect can last for over a week and helps build and easy-going and respectful rapport, where the other person hangs on to your every word.

Work this ritual on any Tuesday or Thursday. Perform the ritual during the Second Hour of the Night. If possible, perform on a Tuesday or Thursday that happens to be a full moon. If not possible, any Tuesday or Thursday will work well enough. Perform the usual purification and protection, and then say:

"AY-OWE-TH, AY-OO-TH, AH-OTH, hear me, as I say the name AY-OWE-TH, AY-OO-TH, AH-OTH, the one who makes the gods lie down, who brings demons forth and compels angels to complete their work. Hear me as I call AY EH EE EYE OH YOU EYE AY YOEH EH AY OO OH YEH EE OO EYE AH. This is the name that answers, and this is the name I have called.

I call on you, great angel Neboun of this hour. By the words SOU FIE I call on the great God Anubis to watch over this ritual.

I call to you, great angel Neboun. I ask that you create a warm rapport with _____."

You now name the person. Describe to Neboun, in your own words, how you want this rapport to feel. Keep it brief and clear.

Then say, "Great angel Neboun, I give thanks for your help. As you came in peace, go in peace."

Create Rapport with a Group

This ritual helps you to be respected and liked by a group of people. You might be going to a party, a conference or just your usual workplace. The ritual works best when aimed at one specific planned event, rather than as a general ritual.

Aim to work this ritual on any night when the moon is waxing or full. Perform the ritual during the Twelfth Hour of the Night. If your planned event occurs during a waning moon, try to plan ahead and perform the ritual long in advance, when the moon is still waxing or full. If that's absolutely impossible, or if it's short notice, you can work the ritual during a waning moon, but do so on a Sunday. (The twelfth hour of a Sunday night will actually fall on a Monday.) Perform the usual purification and protection, and then say:

"AY-OWE-TH, AY-OO-TH, AH-OTH, hear me, as I say the name AY-OWE-TH, AY-OO-TH, AH-OTH, the one who makes the gods lie down, who brings demons forth and compels angels to complete their work. Hear me as I call AY EH EE EYE OH YOU EYE AY YOEH EH AY OO OH YEH EE OO EYE AH. This is the name that answers, and this is the name I have called.

I call on you, great angel Arbrathiabri of this hour. By the words AER THAWEH I call on the great God Sobeck to watch over this ritual.

I call to you, great angel Arbrathiabri. I ask that you create a warm rapport with _____."

Now name the group in a way that is meaningful to you, and specify the time. That might be, 'Jim's friends at the work dance,' or, 'The Management Team from SuperCorporation on Friday afternoon.' The angel will know what you mean. Everything filters through you, so if the name you give the group works for you, it works for the angel. Describe to Arbrathiabri, in your words, how you want this rapport to feel. Keep it brief and clear. Then say, "Great angel Arbrathiabri, I give thanks for your help. As you came in peace, go in peace."

Create Trust with an Individual

Trust is not the same as rapport. Trust means that the individual will trust what you say, regardless of how you act (within reason). This can be used to cover your tracks, to distract or misdirect, and to mislead, or it can be used to make a friendship or relationship more trusting when you feel it's being held back by mistrust.

You can work this ritual on any day, but a full moon can give the magick extra power. Work on the Ninth Hour of the Day. Perform the usual purification and protection, and then say:

"AY-OWE-TH, AY-OO-TH, AH-OTH, hear me, as I say the name AY-OWE-TH, AY-OO-TH, AH-OTH, the one who makes the gods lie down, who brings demons forth and compels angels to complete their work. Hear me as I call AY EH EE EYE OH YOU EYE AY YOEH EH AY OO OH YEH EE OO EYE AH. This is the name that answers, and this is the name I have called.

I call on you, great angel Thymenphree of this hour. By the words PHAYUS PHOE OOTH I call on the great God Horus to watch over this ritual.

I call to you, great angel Thymenphree. I ask that you compel _____ to trust me."

Name the individual, and talk briefly about the nature of the trust. Don't talk about secrets you want to hide. Focus on how strong and deep the trust should be. As always, be clear and brief, direct and sincere.

Then say, "Great angel Thymenphree, I give thanks for your help. As you came in peace, go in peace."

Create Trust with a Group

When you want a group of people to trust you, work this ritual. It works even when that group has come to doubt and suspect you. It won't make people like you, but it will stop them being suspicious and mistrustful of you.

Work this ritual on a Wednesday during a waning moon, at the Tenth Hour of the Day. Perform the usual purification and protection, and then say:

"AY-OWE-TH, AY-OO-TH, AH-OTH, hear me, as I say the name AY-OWE-TH, AY-OO-TH, AH-OTH, the one who makes the gods lie down, who brings demons forth and compels angels to complete their work. Hear me as I call AY EH EE EYE OH YOU EYE AY YOEH EH AY OO OH YEH EE OO EYE AH. This is the name that answers, and this is the name I have called.

I call on you, great angel Sarnokoibal of this hour. By the words BES BYKEY I call on the great God Thoth to watch over this ritual.

I call to you, great angel Sarnokoibal. I ask that you compel _____ to trust me."

Name the group in a way that is meaningful to you. You might say, "The people in marketing," or "Everybody from Tim's friendship group." Speak to the angel about the way you want this trust to feel, in your own words, briefly and clearly.

Then say, "Great angel Sarnokoibal, I give thanks for your help. As you came in peace, go in peace."

Convince Somebody Easily

There's already a ritual to change somebody's mind, but this ritual is used when you're directly trying to convince somebody. You may have been having a long, drawn-out argument, or it could be that you plan to convince somebody to go along with a new idea. Whether you want to suggest marriage, divorce, a business idea or something much smaller, this ritual will do the job. But it only works when you actively speak to the person within the week after the ritual and attempt to convince them of your ideas.

Ideally, work this ritual on a Thursday during a waxing moon, at the Third Hour of the Day. If that's impossible, you can get reasonable results on any day, but avoid Sundays and full moons. Perform the usual purification and protection, and then say:

"AY-OWE-TH, AY-OO-TH, AH-OTH, hear me, as I say the name AY-OWE-TH, AY-OO-TH, AH-OTH, the one who makes the gods lie down, who brings demons forth and compels angels to complete their work. Hear me as I call AY EH EE EYE OH YOU EYE AY YOEH EH AY OO OH YEH EE OO EYE AH. This is the name that answers, and this is the name I have called.

I call on you, great angel Lemnay of this hour. By the words AMEK RAN EBB ECHEEO THOW EETH I call on the great God Apophis to watch over this ritual.

I call to you, great angel Lemnay. I ask that you give me the power to convince _____.

Name the person that you want to convince, and tell Lemnay what it is that you want to convey to the individual. If you know when this will happen, name the time, but this is not essential.

Then say, "Great angel Lemnay, I give thanks for your help. As you came in peace, go in peace."

Convince a Group Easily

When you're making a presentation, talking to a group or in any situation where you need a group of people to accept your message, use this ritual. It will make you more convincing and will make them more susceptible to your words. It doesn't work so well with emails and visual presentations; it relies on the spoken word and your physical presence in the room.

Ideally, work this ritual during a New Moon, at the Seventh Hour of the Day. If you need to use this at short notice and can't wait for a New Moon, work on a Sunday. Perform the usual purification and protection, and then say:

"AY-OWE-TH, AY-OO-TH, AH-OTH, hear me, as I say the name AY-OWE-TH, AY-OO-TH, AH-OTH, the one who makes the gods lie down, who brings demons forth and compels angels to complete their work. Hear me as I call AY EH EE EYE OH YOU EYE AY YOEH EH AY OO OH YEH EE OO EYE AH. This is the name that answers, and this is the name I have called.

I call on you, great angel Orbeth of this hour. By the words OUMES THAWTH I call on the great God Kanum to watch over this ritual.

I call to you, great angel Orbeth. I ask that you give me the power to convince _____.

Name the group in a way that is meaningful to you. Tell Orbeth what it is that you want to convey to this group. Use your own sincere words to describe the result you desire.

Then say, "Great angel Orbeth, I give thanks for your help. As you came in peace, go in peace."

Make Somebody Care About You

This works in established relationships, work relationships, or in situations where the person is currently indifferent to you. It doesn't make you liked, loved or attractive, but it makes the other person care about you, your wellbeing and your desires. This is more useful than you might think, and can be like dynamite when employed at the right time.

Work at the Eleventh Hour of a Wednesday Night, during any time except a New Moon. Perform the usual purification and protection, and then say:

"AY-OWE-TH, AY-OO-TH, AH-OTH, hear me, as I say the name AY-OWE-TH, AY-OO-TH, AH-OTH, the one who makes the gods lie down, who brings demons forth and compels angels to complete their work. Hear me as I call AY EH EE EYE OH YOU EYE AY YOEH EH AY OO OH YEH EE OO EYE AH. This is the name that answers, and this is the name I have called.

I call on you, great angel Bathiabel of this hour. By the words MOU RAPH I call on the great God Thoth to watch over this ritual.

I call to you, great angel Bathiabel. I ask that you make _____ care about me."

Talk to Bathiabel in your own words, describing how you want this to feel, and how deep you want this caring to be. Don't say why or explain your need. Just say what you want.

Then say, "Great angel Bathiabel, I give thanks for your help. As you came in peace, go in peace."

Make Somebody Find You Attractive

You can use this as a love ritual, but also to gain power over others. If somebody is powering over you at work, for example, making them find you attractive can subtly undermine that power.

Work at the Fifth Hour of the Day on a Thursday, during a waxing or full moon. Perform the usual purification and protection, and then say:

"AY-OWE-TH, AY-OO-TH, AH-OTH, hear me, as I say the name AY-OWE-TH, AY-OO-TH, AH-OTH, the one who makes the gods lie down, who brings demons forth and compels angels to complete their work. Hear me as I call AY EH EE EYE OH YOU EYE AY YOEH EH AY OO OH YEH EE OO EYE AH. This is the name that answers, and this is the name I have called.

I call on you, great angel Nouphiair of this hour. By the words ENPHAN COUPH I call on the great God Typhon to watch over this ritual.

I call to you, great angel Nouphiair. I ask that _____ is enflamed with attraction for me."

Tell Nouphiair how you want the person to think and feel about you.

Then say, "Great angel Nouphiair, I give thanks for your help. As you came in peace, go in peace."

Make Somebody See You as a Leader

Need a promotion, or just need more power over somebody else, or respect from those who think you are weak and aimless? Being seen as a leader gets you places. This ritual can be aimed at groups, but that waters it down, so it's best aimed at an individual. If you really want to make a whole group see you as a leader, work the ritual for each member of the group. The ritual can be worked on many days, so you could work for ten days in a row and influence ten different people in a group.

Work this ritual on any day during a waning moon, at the Eight Hour of the Night. Perform the usual purification and protection, and then say:

"AY-OWE-TH, AY-OO-TH, AH-OTH, hear me, as I say the name AY-OWE-TH, AY-OO-TH, AH-OTH, the one who makes the gods lie down, who brings demons forth and compels angels to complete their work. Hear me as I call AY EH EE EYE OH YOU EYE AY YOEH EH AY OO OH YEH EE OO EYE AH. This is the name that answers, and this is the name I have called.

I call on you, great angel Panmoath of this hour. By the words DIA TIPHEH I call on the great God Ahpis to watch over this ritual.

I call to you, great angel Panmoath. I ask that _____ sees me as a great leader.'

In your own words, briefly, tell Panmoath how you want to be seen, and how you want the named individual to feel about you. Describe the leadership qualities you expect them to see in you.

Then say, "Great angel Panmoath, I give thanks for your help. As you came in peace, go in peace."

Sow the Seeds of Doubt

When you want somebody to doubt themselves, or have doubts about a person or situation, this ritual works quickly. If your friend hooks up with somebody that you loathe, you can sour that budding relationship with doubt. If your partner makes plans that repulse you, bring about doubt, so that you get your way. This ritual has many uses, and works best when aimed at one issue, with one individual.

Work this ritual during the First Hour of the Night on a Wednesday when the moon is waning. Perform the usual purification and protection, and then say:

"AY-OWE-TH, AY-OO-TH, AH-OTH, hear me, as I say the name AY-OWE-TH, AY-OO-TH, AH-OTH, the one who makes the gods lie down, who brings demons forth and compels angels to complete their work. Hear me as I call AY EH EE EYE OH YOU EYE AY YOEH EH AY OO OH YEH EE OO EYE AH. This is the name that answers, and this is the name I have called.

I call on you, great angel Menebane of this hour. By the words FARAH COWNETH I call on the great God Bast to watch over this ritual.

I call to you, great angel Menebane. I ask that you bring doubt to the mind of _____."

Name the person, and describe the situation you want to disrupt. Describe what the individual currently believes, and how you want that situation to be filled with doubt.

Then say, "Great angel Menebane, I give thanks for your help. As you came in peace, go in peace."

Create Loyalty

Many people come and go, but there are some people that should be loyal to you, in personal relationships, in business, and in social situations. When you doubt somebody, create loyalty. When a friendship develops, and you need more from that person, create loyalty.

Work this ritual on the Fourth Hour of the Day on a Saturday. The best time of the month is during the last few days of a waning moon or a New Moon. Perform the usual purification and protection, and then say:

"AY-OWE-TH, AY-OO-TH, AH-OTH, hear me, as I say the name AY-OWE-TH, AY-OO-TH, AH-OTH, the one who makes the gods lie down, who brings demons forth and compels angels to complete their work. Hear me as I call AY EH EE EYE OH YOU EYE AY YOEH EH AY OO OH YEH EE OO EYE AH. This is the name that answers, and this is the name I have called.

I call on you, great angel Mormoth of this hour. By the words SENTH EHNIPS I call on the great God Kepera to watch over this ritual.

I call to you, great angel Mormoth. I ask that you make _____ loyal to me.'

Name the person, and in your own words, tell the angel the depth and quality of the loyalty you wish to instill.

Then say, "Great angel Mormoth, I give thanks for your help. As you came in peace, go in peace."

The Timing of the Calls

You've read the rituals, and now you need to know how to calculate the correct planetary hours for your ritual.

When you perform your magick at the right phase of the moon, at the right hour, with the right words, you've got the right ingredients for magick. If you're having a party, you'd probably invite people to turn up at 8pm on a Friday night, because they're more likely to turn up, right? You could send out invitations for a 5am Monday morning party, but people wouldn't show up. Timing isn't everything, and in some magick it scarcely matters at all, but for *this* style of magick, it's a big part of what you're doing. You can go super-obsessive with this, getting the right season, month and all that sort of detail, but I've never found those details to matter. Work with the moon, the days and the hours and the correspondences shown in this book, and you'll get results no matter what time of year it is.

You need to get used to the notion of planetary hours. There are many ways to work out the planetary hours, but the one that applies to this magick might not be the same as others you've used. (Don't use astrology apps that predict planetary hours, as there are many different interpretations of exactly what a planetary hour is. If you find an app that describes this exact method, cool. Otherwise, use Google and a calculator.) In this book, you work by assuming that there are 12 planetary hours between sunrise and sunset, and 12 planetary hours between sunset and sunrise. What follows may sound complicated, but just keep remembering that it was used by the ancients, and they managed without the help of the internet.

Daylight is split into twelve equal 'hours,' and nighttime is split into twelve equal 'hours.' These planetary hours, as they are called, aren't quite the same as normal hours, so you need to do some calculations. The math is not difficult, so don't get hung up on it. It's not rocket science. Seriously, two minutes of Googling and a bit of work with a calculator will get you the answer. Here are the steps.

Step 1: Find out what time the sun rises and sets for the day you want to work. Just Google it. You can find accurate sunrise and sunset times in about ten seconds. You can even find out the times for next week or next month.

Step 2. Work out how many minutes of daylight there are. If the sun rises at 5.55am and sets at 6.15pm, there are 12 hours (between 6am and 6pm), plus 5 minutes before 6am, and 15 minutes after 6pm. So turn the hours into minutes, which is 12 x 60, and that gives you 720. You then add the extra minutes; so that's 720 +5 +15. Altogether that's 740 daylight minutes Might sound complicated, but it isn't. Get this right and your magick is lined up to work. If it's difficult for you, there are some websites that will actually tell you the total number of daylight minutes for the place you live and the day you choose. Google is your friend.

Step 3. Now you've got the number of minutes in the day, you divide that by 12. So here we have 740 divided by 12, which gives us 61.6. That means a planetary hour in this day is 61.66 minutes long. Sometimes planetary hours are much shorter or much longer than a normal hour.

Step 4. If you're working in the first planetary hour, that's easy. You just work any time in the first 61.66 minutes after sunrise. But what about the other hours? If you're looking to find the time for the eighth hour, you work out what time it is when the seventh hour ends. For any hour, just work out how many hours have passed *before it starts*. For the eleventh hour, you'd add up ten planetary hours. For the fifth hour, you'd add up four planetary hours. Here, we want the eighth hour, so we work out seven planetary hours. So that's 61.66 multiplied by 7. The answer is 431.62.

Step 5. You now know that your eighth planetary hour starts 431.62 minutes after sunrise. So what time is that? You need to convert that last number to normal hours again. So that's 431.62 divided by 60. That gives you 7.19 normal hours. You now know that your allotted hour starts 7.19 hours after sunrise.

Step 6. This is the final step. 7 normal hours after 5.55am is 12.55pm. That's easy. But the number you had was 7.19 hours, so you need to know how long .19 of an hour is. You do this by multiplying it by 60. So .19 multiplied by 60 is 11.4. So now add 11.4 minutes to 12.55pm. To make it easier, round it down and just add 11 minutes. Your final answer is 1.06pm.

Because you've done a little bit of rounding here and there, it makes sense to wait a few minutes after the planetary hour starts. So if I'd done that calculation, and worked out a starting time of 1.06pm, I'd aim for 1.15pm, so that the correct hour is well underway. That would still give me plenty of time to get the ritual done before the 61.6 minutes are over.

If you've read all that and think it looks like the most complicated and mind-boggling math, remember that ordinary people were doing this sort of thing millennia ago. You can get this right. I know this is going to stress some of you out, so here's another example.

It's December in New York, and you want to work during the fourth planetary hour. Your first job is to work out how long the hours are on this particular day. You get on Google and search for sunrise and sunset times for today, in New York. It tells you that today in New York the sun rises at 6am and sets at 6.15pm. You know that's exactly 12 hours and 15 minutes. Now comes the easy math. There are 60 minutes in every hour, and 12 hours of daylight, so that's 60 multiplied by 12. Using your calculator, you find that's 720. Don't forget to add the extra 15 minutes. That gives you 735 minutes of daylight. Divide that by 12, and you've now worked out that each planetary hour today lasts exactly 61.25 minutes. Easy. You want to perform the ritual sometime during the fourth planetary hour. The fourth hour starts *when the third hour ends,* so work out how long 3 planetary hours are. That's 61.25 multiplied by 3, which gives you 183.75. You now know that your fourth hour starts 183.75 minutes after sunrise. So convert that back to normal time by dividing 183.75 by 60. That gives you 3.06 normal hours. Three hours after the 6am sunrise is 9am. But what about that .06? Multiply that by 60, to get 3.6. Which means your fourth planetary hour starts about three and a half minutes after nine. Aim to start at ten past nine and you'll be in the right hour, with lots of time to spare.

If you're good at math, forgive the basic explanation. Most folks don't have a stress-free time with math. If you're crap at math, and that sounds way too complicated, take it easy and work through it step by step. It's easy and it's worth taking the time to get it right.

Remember as well that if you're asked to work on the eleventh hour of a Tuesday night, that's actually going to be Wednesday morning. To get it right, just follow the instructions and count from the allocated time you've been given. If it says the Third Hour of the day on a Wednesday, you know that's the third hour of Wednesday morning. If it's the sixth hour of a Monday night, then it might fall late on Monday night or early Tuesday morning. If it's the Twelfth Hour of a Thursday Night, you know that's going to be early Friday morning. Just calculate from sunset on the Thursday and you'll get it right.

Life can get in the way of this magick. You might be told to work during the Third Hour of the day on a Thursday, but you're at work. Are you meant to perform the ritual under your desk? Do the best you can to work at the right time. If you can't, try the closest alternative. In this case, try the Third Hour of the *Night* on a Thursday. In most of the rituals, there is some flexibility. Do your best to stay within these guidelines. If it's all absolutely impossible, then try the Demonic Influence magick instead, as that has no time restrictions.

Now for some notes on pronunciation. In the ritual, you see words like AY-OWE-TH and YOEH. It's all easy to say if you study this pronunciation guide.

AY is like MAY without M.

OWE is the word OWE.

TH is like the end of BETH.

OO is the sound in the middle of MOON.

AH is like the AH sound in FATHER.

EH is the E sound in MET.

EE is like SEE without S.

EYE, OH, YOU are just the words you'd expect them to be. (You may notice that at some points in the ritual it sounds like you're reciting a list of vowels: A, E, I, O, U. This is because some of the phrases are created around the standard vowels. You don't need to know that, but it's interesting!) YOEH is like the YO you get in YO-YO, or the YO! that rappers use. You follow that with the EH sound, which is like the middle of MET. YEH is like YET without the T.

The Magick of the Hours

The relevant angels, words, and Gods of each hour are presented in the rituals. Here, I set them out with the correct pronunciation, so that you can become familiar with them before you attempt the ritual.

In some traditions, there are different correspondences for the night and for the day. Here, you can use these angels, words, and Gods for the day and the night. So the third hour of the day is, in this system, almost identical to the third hour of the night. Use the recommended hour where you can, but if not, swap day for night and night for day.

When it comes to pronunciation, you see AH used all the time, and this is the AH you get in FATHER. The rest is explained, or should be fairly clear. You don't have to learn this all at once. Use it when you need it.

The First Hour

The Angel of the First Hour is Menebane, pronounced MEN-EBB-AIN. That's the word MEN, the word EBB and PAIN without the P.

The words of the First Hour are FARAH COWNETH. FARAH is FAR and AH, and then you've got COW, and NETH which is like METH but with N.

The great God of the First Hour is Bast. That's pronounced like BASTARD without ARD.

The Second Hour

The Angel of the Second Hour is Neboun, pronounced NE-BOUN. That's like NET without the T, and BOUND without the D.

The words of the Second Hour are SOU FIE, which you say like SOUP without P. FIE is like PIE but with F.

The great God of the Second hour is Anubis, pronounced here as ANNE-YOU-BISS.

The Third Hour

The Angel of the Third Hour is Lemnay, pronounced LEM-NEIGH. That's the first part of LEMON and the word NEIGH.

The words of the Third Hour are AMEK RAN EBB ECHEEO THOW EETH. AMEK, RAN and EBB are obvious. ECHEEO is like ECHO, but with EE in the middle, so you get something like EK-EE-OH. THOW is like THROW without the R. EETH is TEETH without the T.

The great God of the Third Hour is Apophis, pronounced APP-OH-FISS. The first two sounds are easy, and FISS is like FIST without T.

The Fourth Hour

The Angel of the Fourth Hour is Mormoth, pronounced MORE-MOTH. If you need help with that pronunciation, I give up.

The words of the Fourth Hour are SENTH EHNIPS. SENTH is like TENTH with T. For EHNIPS, EHN is like TEN without T. IPS is like HIPS without H. Together you get EHNIPS.

The great God of the Fourth Hour is Kepera, pronounced KEP-EH-RAH. KEP is like KEN but with P at the end. EH is like the E sound in MET. RAH is said the way you'd imagine.

The Fifth Hour

The Angel of the Fifth Hour is Nouphiair, pronounced NOU-FEE-AIR. NOU rhymes with YOU. FEE and AIR are obvious.

The words of the Fifth Hour are ENPHAN COUPH. ENPH is like the first part of ENFLAME, and then you put AN at the end. COUPH sounds like COOL with F at the end, instead of L.

36

The great God of the Fifth Hour is Typhon, pronounced TIE-FON. TIE is obvious, and FON rhymes with GONE.

The Sixth Hour

The Angel of the Sixth Hour is Corborbath, pronounced CORE-BORE-BAH-TH. CORE and BORE are obvious. BAH is like the word AH, but with a B sound at the front. (Think of Bah Bah Black Sheep.) TH is the sound you get at the end of NORTH.

The words of the Sixth Hour are BAI SOL BAI, pronounced BAY SOLL BYE.

The great God of the Sixth Hour is Sekmet, pronounced SECK-MET, which should be obvious.

The Seventh Hour

The Angel of the Seventh Hour is Orbeth, pronounced ORB-EH-ETH. ORB is as you'd imagine. EH is the E sound from MET. ETH is like BETH without the B.

The words of the Seventh Hour are OUMES THAWTH. OUMES is pronounced OO-MESS. THAWTH is clearly the word THAW with TH at the end.

The great God of the Seventh Hour is Kanum, pronounced KAH-NUMB. You should be getting the hang of these pronunciations by now.

The Eighth Hour

The Angel of the Eighth Hour is Panmoath, pronounced PAN-MOW-AHTH. PAN and MOW are obvious. AHTH is the sound of the word AH, with TH at the end.

The words of the Eighth Hour are DIA TIPHEH. DIA is like DEE-AH. TIPH is like TIFF. EH is the E sounds from MET.

The great God of the Eighth Hour is Ahpis, pronounced AH-PIZZ.

The Ninth Hour

The Angel of the Ninth Hour is Thymenphree, pronounced THIGH-MEN-FREE. It doesn't get much easier than that.

The words of the Ninth Hour are PHAYUS PHOE OOTH. PHAYUS is like FAY and US. PHOE is said like FOE. OOTH is like TOOTH without the T.

The great God of the Ninth Hour is Horus, pronounced HOAR-USS.

The Tenth Hour

The Angel of the Tenth Hour is Sarnokoibal, pronounced SAR-NO-COE-EE-BAL.

The words of the Tenth Hour are BES BYKEY, pronounced BESS BYE-KEY.

The great God of the Tenth Hour is Thoth, pronounced as THAWTH. That's the words THAW with a TH sound at the end.

The Eleventh Hour

The Angel of the Eleventh Hour is Bathiabel, pronounced BAHTH-EE-AH-BELL. BAHTH is the BAH sound discussed earlier, with the TH sound at the end. The rest should be obvious.

The words of the Eleventh Hour are MOU RAPH. MOU is pronounced MOW-OU. MOW is just MOW, and OU is the word YOU without the Y. RAPH is RAHPH, so that's the AH sound with R at the front and F at the end.

The great God of the Eleventh Hour is Thoth, here pronounced THOOTH, which is like TOOTH, but you put TH at either end of the word.

The Twelfth Hour

The Angel of the Twelfth Hour is Arbrathiabri, which is pronounced ARB-RAHTH-EE-AH-BREE. ARB is like CARB without the C. RAHTH is the AH sound, with R at the beginning and ending with TH. The rest is obvious.

The words of the Twelfth Hour are AER THAWEH. AER is pronounced AH-AIR. THAWEH is the word THAW, ending with the E sound from MET.

The great God of the Twelfth Hour is Sobeck, pronounced SOW-BECK. (That's sow as in sowing seed, rather than a female pig.)

Part 2: Demonic Influence

In the next few chapters, you find rituals that call on the demons of the Goetia, to influence others in accordance with your wishes. If you read much about these demons you'll get confused, upset, opinionated, bored or dispirited. Try the magick instead. It's good stuff and it doesn't need to be too convoluted.

Whenever anybody publishes a book on Goetic technique, there's often a bit of an uproar about which sources were used, how words are pronounced and all those boring aspects of magick. If you have your own opinions, your own ideas, and if you insist that they are right, then use your own sigils and words in these rituals. You can adapt it if you want to, but it's easier to work with what I give you here.

A few years ago, Jason Miller upset the pompous snobs of the occult world by creating a mini-wealth spell that called on the Goetic demon Bune. I call it a spell because it read more like witchcraft than ritual magick. His spell did away with the lengthy preparation, equipment, and ritual madness that accompanies most Goetic evocations. The catch? No demon appears. It's not an evocation but a way of tasking the demon. But people liked it, found it worked well enough, so long as you didn't ask for too much. It was so damned simple, there was nothing to stop you having a go. Gordon Winterfield was more ritualistic in his attack book, using a sigil along with a call, but without much ceremony or altered consciousness. Both approaches are somewhat like a chaos magician's interpretation of Geotic ritual; you stew it down to the bare bones and get it so simple that it's *almost* too simple, but still just about good enough to work.

With respect, I will say that the problem for me with Miller's working was that it was just a bunch of words. Words can work, course they can. But with the Goetic demons, are words enough? And does the demon know it's being called? Ever heard a room full of occultists talk about a demon? Probably not, because most discussions now happen on the occult forums of the internet. (Can anything good come of those forums? Yeah. You get good advice, once a decade or so. But mostly you get egos and claims and anger. If you want my advice – and you probably don't - I'd say that every minute spent in an occult forum would be better spent reading a magick book or doing magick. Or, you know, eating cake. Discussing occultism with a bunch of angry kids is less useful than candle magic. Ha!)

But if you are ever in the real world with real occultists, ask them how to pronounce Bune. You'll hear BOON, BOON-AH, BOON-EH, BOU'N, and many variations, including BEAM, BIMAY and more. How's the demon meant to know you mean Bune, the mighty Duke, 26th spirit of the Goetia? Will it really hear? Maybe, but this is why I think you should use a sigil too. Miller's work was cool, and a mini-revolution, but I'd have preferred it to be more than just a call. The Goetic demons like to have more than that.

Winterfield uses sigils, but not much in the way of magickal consciousness. Although I have respect for Miller and Winterfield, what I'm giving you here is, I hope, a bit more meaty without being dull, boring, laborious, or requiring a trip to the local occult store.

For a good result, I think you need a ritual structure, a name, a personally drawn sigil, and a mild magickal state of conscious. You also need to reward the spirit with a sacrifice. The sacrifice never involves animals because, despite what some people tell you, that's just a waste of animals. Instead, you reward the demon by sacrificing your own comfort. We'll come to that later.

I also believe that in any Goetic ritual, the spirit's name should be the first thing you say. In lots of magick (including the first half of this book), you see phrases like, 'I call on thee oh mighty and grand, gracious spirit, Bune,' but Bune wasn't listening until you said his name. That means everything else before the spirit's name is just noise. If you 're at a party, and your friend Peter is busy in conversation with somebody, you don't mutter, 'I'd really like it if you could get me a drink, Peter.' Peter only turns around when you say Peter. If you say, 'Peter, could you get me a drink,' clearly, then Peter hears the whole sentence, and maybe he gets you the drink. Maybe not, but at least he's listening. Everything here starts with the spirit's name, and then comes back to it after other convincing statements and actions are put in there to get the spirit on your side and under your command. Yes, it is possible to achieve both at once, and you should. There's a bunch of occultists that believe you should call on the demons without protection and without using divine names, because that's going to piss the demons off. If you want to experiment with that, I'll leave you to it, but in this book, I nod to tradition by using divine names and angels to constrain the demons.

I think it works better and it keeps everything under control. If you give a demon your trust, it might do what you want, but it might not. Better to constrain and command. If you disagree, feel free to omit the divine aspects of the ritual, and good luck to you.

On to the magick.

In the following twelve rituals, you Purify and Protect, as you have been shown. Next, you raise magickal energy as you draw the sigil. You do this purely by chanting the demon's name. This alone should generate a great deal of energy.

For each demon, there is a sigil, illustrated on the page following the ritual description. And if you do your research you'll find there are lots of different sigils for each demon. Google around and you'll find lots of variations on each sigil. Do you need the oldest and most authentic? No – any sigil will do. The demons get used to these sigils. They work.

Get a piece of paper and draw the sigil as best you can. If you think you can't draw, stop whining and draw it! These sigils look like stick drawings. They were scribbled down without much ceremony at all, and they never, ever look the same. You can copy these sigils easily. That is what you do. Don't stop, think you've done a bad job and start again; finish what you begin, even if there are errors. Your personally drawn sigil is better than something in a book. So copy out what is in this book, in your own hand, without tracing it. As you draw, you chant the demon's name over and over. Focus on getting into a magickal state of mind as you do this, rather than on the quality of your drawing.

The sigils do not have to be perfect. As I said earlier, if you look around, the sigils look different in just about every book you read. They still work.

You are then instructed to place your hand drawn sigil before you. It can be on the floor, or in your hand. It should be within the circle, and it should be visible.

You then make the call as instructed in each chapter, and chant the name until you feel the demon's presence. That can happen instantly. You might have felt a cool spread of air on your back, or a tingling in your skin, or a pull in your mind, as soon as you said the demon's name. Or it may take much longer. Keep chanting until you sense the demon. Reach out for it with your mind. What you sense may be quite vague, a mere shift in the atmosphere. If you feel anything at all, recognize that as the demon, and continue. If you feel absolutely nothing, and you are certain nothing has changed, end the ritual and try again another time.

You are not evoking the demon to appear. Do not expect to see or hear the demon. You may, but it's not likely and it's not expected. But it is expected that you will *sense* the demon. Scents, sounds, anything that feels or seems in any way strange or supernatural should be taken as a sign. If you suspect you have contact, continue with the ritual. To ignore it is to jeopardize your future connection with this spirit.

You then speak words as instructed, using your own phrases, and eventually dismiss the demon, then step out of your circle and go back to normality. When you speak to the demon, keep it short and to the point. Never justify your actions. Never explain the reasons. Just say what you want.

Each ritual calls on the demon, then the divine name IAO (pronounced EE-AH-OH), followed by the constraining angel that corresponds to the demon. This is followed by the name of three angels that are also bound to the demon. These are all spelled phonetically, and by now you should know how to read these. Read the words as though they are English. So for BARK-EE-ELL, it's obviously the word BARK, the EE sound (from SEE), and ELL, which rhymes with HELL. It's only difficult if you worry about it.

You close the ritual by offering a sacrifice, or as I prefer to call it, a reward. This means that you go to the trouble of suffering some discomfort, some loss of time – something that makes you feel like you have paid the price – and you offer this to the demon. I have listed the main rewards that the demons want. If a demon favors hunger, then you promise to reward the demon with an afternoon or day of hunger. Then, when you get what you wished for, you must go hungry for an afternoon (or whatever you promised). If a demon favors honor, that means the demon wants you to spread words about its deed. Make sure you publicly declare the workings of the demon. If a demon favors pain, then you can offer up your own personal anguish over a memory, or any physical pain you happen to experience. (It would be irresponsible of me to suggest you actually cause yourself pain!)

Making this offer is easy. You tell the demon what you offer, and that is all. When you get what you asked for, there is no need to call the demon. The demon is waiting for its reward. As soon as you can, and definitely within a few days, you offer the reward. You do not need to perform this ritualistically. Don't call the demon to come back. Just experience the sacrifice. Feel the hunger, the pain, or spread the word about the demon.

When you're performing the ritual, only offer what you are truly happy to give. That is vital.

When the ritual is complete, step out of the circle, and get back to normal. Keep the sigil in a safe place. If you call on the demon again, draw the sigil anew. This may mean that you create quite a collection of sigils. This is true, but I prefer not to burn or damage sigils, as this burning technique is a traditional way of punishing the demons. So protect the sigils in a safe place. If you must dispose of them, wrap them all in black cloth and bury them where they will not be disturbed.

If you're familiar with the occult, you may want to banish as soon as the ritual is over. I don't see any need to banish, but if you do, use your banishing of choice. For best results, wait an hour or so, if you dare, before banishing. If you don't know what banishing is, don't worry about it. You've dismissed the demon, and that is good enough.

Make Somebody Shut Their Mouth

This ritual can be used to make a gossip stop gossiping, or to make a loud and obnoxious person more subdued. It can even be used on a partner, or ex-partner, who is too loose-tongued about your personal life. To make somebody shut their mouth, call on the demon Zagan.

Purify, protect, and draw the sigil of Zagan while chanting the name ZAH-GAN. Place the sigil before you and call:

> "I call on thee, ZAH-GAN.
> In the name of EE-AH-OH,
> I call on the great angel OO-MAH-BELL,
> and the angels of light,
> VAY-DEE-ELL,
> MAHT-ZUF-EVE-AH-ELL and
> BARK-EE-ELL
> to bring forth ZAH-GAN."

Chant ZAH-GAN until you feel the demon's presence. Then say:

"I call on you, Zagan, to shut the mouth of _____.' Name the person, and tell Zagan what kind of silence you want. Do you wish to make a loud person quiet, or shut the lies of a gossip? State this clearly, and then. say, "Go now, Zagan, and know that I will reward you with _____." Name the reward you have chosen. Zagan favors honor. Finish by saying, "As you came in peace, go in peace. You are dismissed."

The Sigil of Zagan

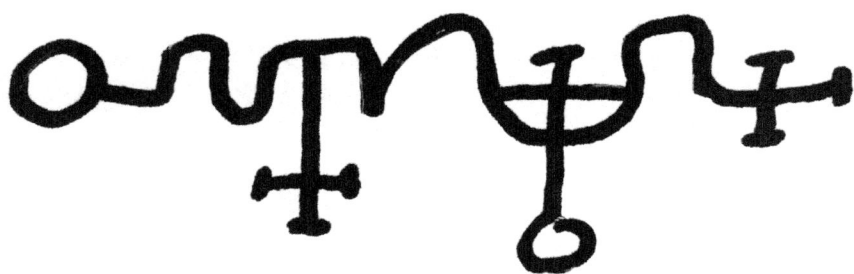

Make a Neighbor Quiet

If your neighbor makes disturbing noise, you need peace. It doesn't matter whether it's music, machinery or loud arguments; this ritual can bring silence. To make a neighbor quiet, call on the demon Orias.

Purify, protect, and draw the sigil of Orias while chanting the name OAR-EE-ASS. Place the sigil before you and call:

"I call on thee, OAR-EE-ASS.
In the name of EE-AH-OH,
I call on the great angel ME-HELL,
and the angels of light,
MAHM-LEE-ELL,
YUH-KAH-LASH-EE-KAH-ELL and
HAH-AH-ZEE-ELL
to bring forth OAR-EE-ASS."

Chant OAR-EE-ASS until you feel the demon's presence. Then say:

"I call on you, Orias, to make _____ quiet.' Name the person, and ask Orias to make that person afraid to make noise. Furthermore, ask the demon to subdue that person, and make them meek. Say, "Go now, Orias, and know that I will reward you with _____." Name the reward you have chosen. Orias favors hunger. Finish by saying, "As you came in peace, go in peace. You are dismissed."

The Sigil of Orias

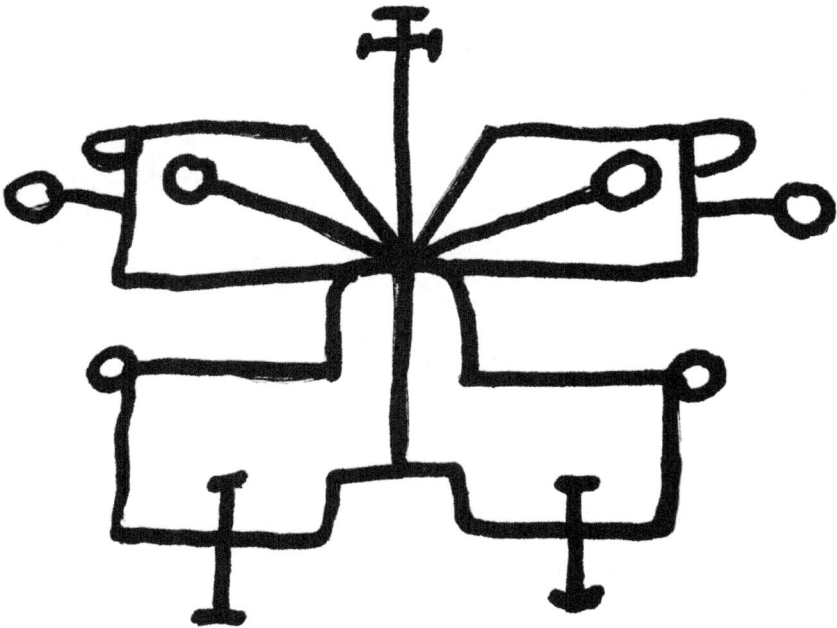

Make a Neighbor Move Away

Some neighbors are such a pain, you need them to leave. To make a neighbor (or even a roommate) move away, call on the demon Sitri.

Purify, protect, and draw the sigil of Sitri while chanting the name SIT-REE. Place the sigil before you and call:

"I call on thee, SIT-REE.
In the name of EE-AH-OH,
I call on the great angel HAH-AH-EE-AH,
and the angels of light,
HAH-VAH-ELL,
HAHN-AVAH-ELL and
AHSH-ASH-EE-ELL
to bring forth SIT-REE."

Chant SIT-REE until you feel the demon's presence. Then say:

"I call on you, Sitri, to make _____ move from this place.' Name the person, and ask Sitri to make the person in question restless, fearful and absolutely desperate to move away. Say, "Go now, Sitri, and know that I will reward you with _____." Name the reward you have chosen. Sitri favors honor. Finish by saying, "As you came in peace, go in peace. You are dismissed."

The Sigil of Sitri

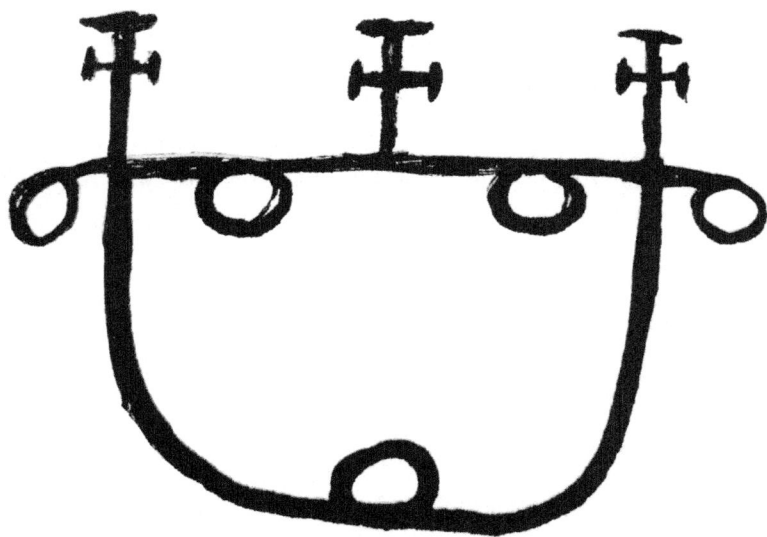

Make Somebody Afraid of You

Fear is power. When somebody is too cocky, rude or unpleasant to be around, you can make them fear you. When you need to control somebody, make them fear you. Do not use this on close friends unless you are willing to damage the friendship. It is best used on associates and people who are in your life by necessity rather than choice. To make somebody afraid of you, call on the demon Forneus.

Purify, protect, and draw the sigil of Forneus while chanting the name FOR-NEE-USS. Place the sigil before you and call:

> "I call on thee, FOR-NEE-USS.
> In the name of EE-AH-OH,
> I call on the great angel OH-MAH-ELL,
> and the angels of light,
> AHSH-FEE-ELL,
> VUH-NAH-DEE-ELL and
> ME-MAH-ELL
> to bring forth FOR-NEE-USS."

Chant FOR-NEE-USS until you feel the demon's presence. Then say:

"I call on you, Forneus, to make _____ fear me.' Name the person, and tell the demon the nature and depth of fear. Do you want the person to be cautious or terrified? Make it clear. Say, "Go now, Forneus, and know that I will reward you with _____." Name the reward you have chosen. Forneus favors pain and hunger. Finish by saying, "As you came in peace, go in peace. You are dismissed."

The Sigil of Forneus

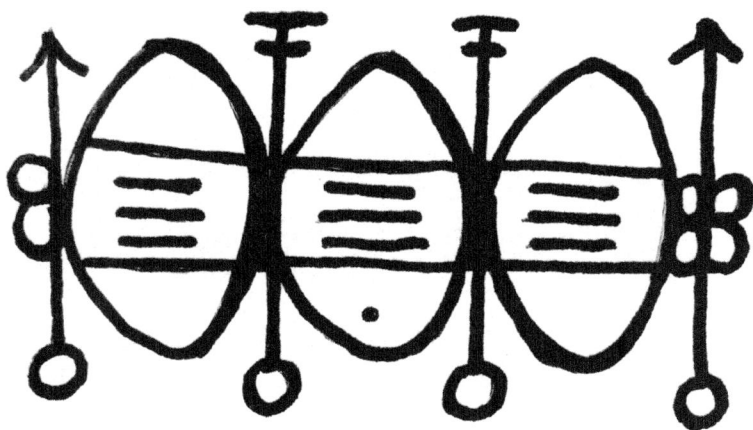

Project Charisma

Charisma can make everybody want to be around you. It can take time to develop this sort of popularity, but if you want to radiate an easy charm, use this ritual. To project charisma, call on the demon Dantaylion.

Purify, protect and draw the sigil of Dantaylion while chanting the name DANT-AY-LEE-ON. Place the sigil before you and call:

> "I call on thee, DANT-AY-LEE-ON.
> In the name of EE-AH-OH,
> I call on the great angel HAY-EE-ELL,
> and the angels of light,
> HACK-TART-EE-ELL,
> YAN-VEE-VAH-ELL and
> YAW-FAK-TEE-ELL
> to bring forth DANT-AY-LEE-ON."

Chant DANT-AY-LEE-ON until you feel the demon's presence. Then say:

"I call on you, Dantaylion, to help me project my personal charisma. Let others see me as bold, bright, humorous and charismatic.' If there is a specific person that you wish to influence with your aura of charisma, tell the demon, briefly and clearly and in your own words. Say, "Go now, Dantaylion, and know that I will reward you with _____." Name the reward you have chosen. Dantaylion favors honor. Finish by saying, "As you came in peace, go in peace. You are dismissed."

The Sigil of Dantaylion

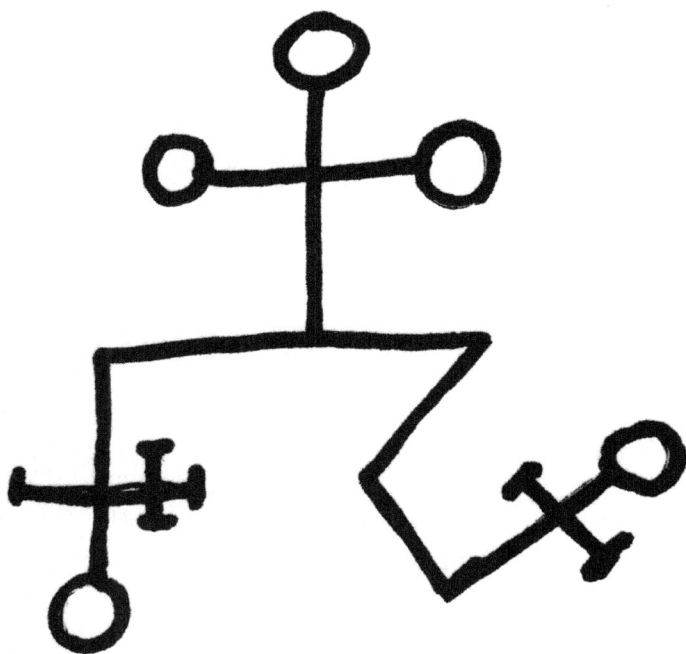

Project Trustworthiness

If you need to appear as though you are trustworthy, regardless of your actual intentions and actions, this ritual can help. To project trustworthiness, call on the demon Ipos.

Purify, protect and draw the sigil of Ipos while chanting the name EE-POSS. Place the sigil before you and call:

"I call on thee, EE-POSS.
In the name of EE-AH-OH,
I call on the great angel YEH-YAY-ELL,
and the angels of light,
YAH-ULAH-YEE-ELL,
YUH-HAW-HEE-ELL and
YAT-ZEE-VAH-ELL
to bring forth EE-POSS."

Chant EE-POSS until you feel the demon's presence. Then say:

"I call on you, Ipos, to make me appear trustworthy." If there is a specific person that you wish to influence with your aura of trustworthiness, tell the demon, briefly and clearly and in your own words. Say, "Go now, Ipos, and know that I will reward you with _____." Name the reward you have chosen. Ipos favors sexual abstinence. Finish by saying, "As you came in peace, go in peace. You are dismissed."

The Sigil of Ipos

Project an Aura of Authority

When people see you as a person in authority, they look up to you, they listen to you, and they try to make things go your way. This is invaluable in relationships and in business. To project an aura of authority, call on the demon Cimeries.

Purify, protect and draw the sigil of Cimeries while chanting the name SIMM-AIR-EES. Place the sigil before you and call:

> "I call on thee, SIMM-AIR-EES.
> In the name of EE-AH-OH,
> I call on the great angel MEN-AH-KELL,
> and the angels of light,
> MEK-EE-ELL,
> NAH-TREE-ELL and
> KUH-DAW-SHE-ELL
> to bring forth SIMM-AIR-EES."

Chant SIMM-AIR-EES until you feel the demon's presence. Then say:

"I call on you, Cimeries, to give me an aura of authority. Make all who see me shudder in awe.' This is not meant literally but creates the right mood and feeling. If there is a specific person that you wish to influence with your aura of authority, tell the demon, briefly and clearly and in your own words. Say, "Go now, Cimeries, and know that I will reward you with _____." Name the reward you have chosen. Cimeries favors sexual abstinence. Finish by saying, "As you came in peace, go in peace. You are dismissed."

The Sigil of Cimeries

Stir Hatred

Hatred can be used to distract, to end relationships, or cause chaos in an organization. Be cautious about where you use this, because if the person you charge with hatred is in your vicinity, you may catch a lot of the flak. You can stir hatred in one person, or make two people hate each other. To stir hatred, call on the demon Furcas.

Purify, protect and draw the sigil of Furcas while chanting the name FUR-CASS. Place the sigil before you and call:

> "I call on thee, FUR-CASS.
> In the name of EE-AH-OH,
> I call on the great angel DAH-KNEE-ELL,
> and the angels of light,
> DOORS-VEE-ELL,
> NAH-SUSS-EE-ELL and
> JAW-FUSS-EE-ELL
> to bring forth FUR-CASS."

Chant FUR-CASS until you feel the demon's presence. Then say:

"I call on you, Furcas, to bring hatred to _____." Name the person or people who you wish to enrage with hate. Let the demon know, briefly and clearly, the nature and depth of the hate. Say, "Go now, Furcas, and know that I will reward you with _____." Name the reward you have chosen. Furcas favors pain and honor. Finish by saying, "As you came in peace, go in peace. You are dismissed."

The Sigil of Furcas

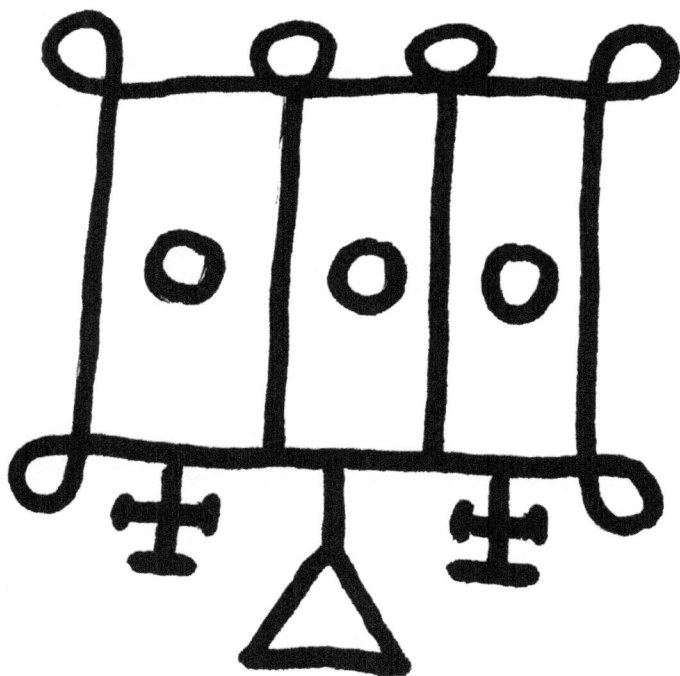

Spread Mistrust

You can make one person mistrustful of another person or organization. You can also make everybody within an organization mistrustful of one another. This causes great disruption. Do not use this when you belong to that organization, or you too will be mistrusted. To spread mistrust, call on the demon Andras.

Purify, protect and draw the sigil of Andras while chanting the name AND-RASS. Place the sigil before you and call:

"I call on thee, AND-RASS.
In the name of EE-AH-OH,
I call on the great angel AH-NOO-ELL,
and the angels of light,
AH-TUTS-AH-MEE-ELL,
NAHT-KEY-ELL and
VAH-TUD-ME-ELL
to bring forth AND-RASS."

Chant AND-RASS until you feel the demon's presence. Then say:

"I call on you, Andras, to spread mistrust _____." Name the person or place in question, and describe to Andras the nature and extent of the mistrust. Let the demon know, briefly and clearly, the people who should become mistrustful, or the place where mistrust should become rife. Say, "Go now, Andras, and know that I will reward you with _____." Name the reward you have chosen. Andras favors honor. Finish by saying, "As you came in peace, go in peace. You are dismissed."

The Sigil of Andras

Create Unease

A subtler approach to disruption is to create unease. This leaves somebody functional, but uneasy, which can make them easier to manipulate and coerce. To create unease, call on the demon Andromalius.

Purify, protect and draw the sigil of Andromalius while chanting the name AND-ROW-MAL-EE-USS. Place the sigil before you and call:

> "I call on thee, AND-ROW-MAL-EE-USS.
> In the name of EE-AH-OH,
> I call on the great angel MOO-ME-AH,
> and the angels of light,
> MAL-KEY-HAH-ELL,
> VENAH-DEETS-VAH-ELL and
> MAH-KUV-ACK-VEE-ELL
> to bring forth AND-ROW-MAL-EE-USS."

Chant AND-ROW-MAL-EE-USS until you feel the demon's presence. Then say:

"I call on you, Andromalius, to bring unease to _____." Name the person or place in question, and describe to Andromalius the nature and extent of the unease you wish to cause. Speak clearly and briefly. Say, "Go now, Andromalius, and know that I will reward you with _____." Name the reward you have chosen. Andromalius favors hunger and discomfort. Finish by saying, "As you came in peace, go in peace. You are dismissed."

The Sigil of Andromalius

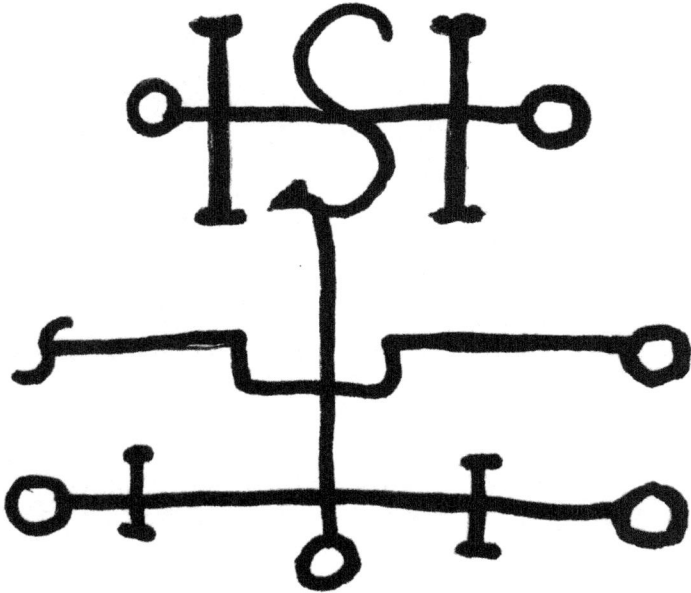

Create Confusion

Confusion can give you the upper hand in many situations. To bring about confusion, call on the demon Naberius.

Purify, protect and draw the sigil of Naberius while chanting the name NAB-AIR-EE-USS. Place the sigil before you and call:

"I call on thee, NAB-AIR-EE-USS.
In the name of EE-AH-OH,
I call on the great angel HAH-VEE-AH,
and the angels of light,
CAH-GEE-ELL,
HAWF-NEE-ELL and
VUSH-AH-AHSH-EE-ELL
to bring forth NAB-AIR-EE-USS."

Chant NAB-AIR-EE-USS until you feel the demon's presence. Then say:

"I call on you, Naberius, to bring great confusion to _____."
Name the person in question, and describe to Naberius the nature and extent of the confusion you wish to cause. Speak clearly and briefly. Say, "Go now, Naberius, and know that I will reward you with _____." Name the reward you have chosen. Naberius favors hunger and sorrow. Finish by saying, "As you came in peace, go in peace. You are dismissed."

Note that in CAH-GEE-ELL, GEE uses the G you hear in GLIMMER rather than the G you hear in GEE WHIZ.

The Sigil of Naberius

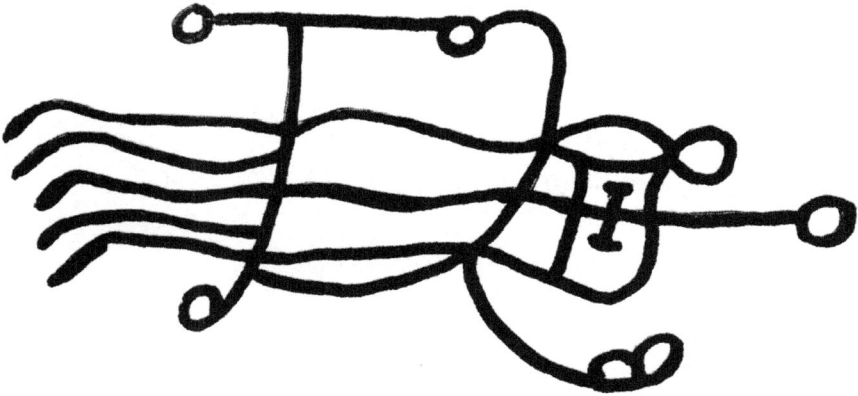

Urge a Confession

When you believe that somebody close to you has lied, or withheld important information that should be shared, you want a confession. This ritual can make people confess their darkest secrets, so be sure you want to know the truth. To urge a confession, call on the demon Andrealphus.

Purify, protect and draw the sigil of Andrealphus while chanting the name AND-REE-AL-FUSS. Place the sigil before you and call:

"I call on thee, AND-REE-AL-FUSS.
In the name of EE-AH-OH,
I call on the great angel DAM-EB-EE-AH,
and the angels of light,
DAWD-NEE-ELL,
MAH-SHUFF-EE-DAH-ELL and
BEE-VAH-ELL
to bring forth AND-REE-AL-FUSS."

Chant AND-REE-AL-FUSS until you feel the demon's presence. Then say:

"I call on you, Andrealphus, to bring forth a confession from _____." Name the person in question, and describe to Andrealphus the nature of the confession you seek. Speak clearly and briefly. Say, "Go now, Andrealphus, and know that I will reward you with _____." Name the reward you have chosen. Andrealphus favors pain and sexual abstinence. Finish by saying, "As you came in peace, go in peace. You are dismissed."

The Sigil of Andrealphus

Influence with Magick

I've tried to write a practical book. It might appear short, but the power you hold within your hands is something that can last you a lifetime, and change your life, sometimes in small ways, and sometimes with great significance. I hope you think it was worth a few dollars, and if you put the magick to use, I am sure it will be.

Writing a book takes more effort than you might believe, with decades of research, months of writing, and a lot of money to get it ready for publication, so please, if you like what you've read, review my book on Amazon or Goodreads. Thank you for your support.

Sincerely,

Corwin Hargrove

Printed in Great Britain
by Amazon